SUMO

A HISTORY OF THE SPORT

JUDAH LYONS

Minute Help Press
ANAHEIM, CALIFORNIA

Contents

About Minute Help

Minute Help Press is building a library of books for people with only minutes to spare. Follow @minutehelp on Twitter to receive the latest information about free and paid publications from Minute Help Press or visit minutehelp.com.

INTRODUCTION

Sumo is the official national sport of Japan, as recognized by the country's government. It is built around the simple concept of two nigh-naked men battling within a small roped ring, but actually has a far deeper meaning, which encompasses both Shinto beliefs and Japan's most subtle cultural nuances.

Historical records have the sport dating back at least 1500 years, with popular myths linking the sport to events even further back than that. Professionalized in the 18th century, sumo continues to thrive in the present-day, staging six tournaments a year with the average weight of competitors around 140 kilograms (308 lbs).

A tournament matchday in Nagoya, 2010

[1]

Sumo In A Nutshell

The basic rules of sumo are incredibly simple. Two combatants, their hair tied in the samurai gingko-leaf form and wearing nothing but a sash around the waist, enter a roped-ring of 4.5 meters' diameter. They crouch down at white starters' lines 80 centimeters apart and leap into action. To win, they must either push an opponent outside the circle or knock them down anywhere. Understandably, given the compact size of the ring and simplicity of rules, most bouts last for a mere few seconds but some epic encounters have continued for six minutes or more. There are currently 82 recognized ways of winning a sumo bout but less than half of them are regularly seen in tournaments. Indeed 12 of those techniques were only added as recently as 2001 in response to the increased agility – and thus more unusual winning styles – introduced by Mongolian wrestlers in particular.

Broadly speaking, there are two main styles of sumo: yotsu, which relies on grabbing an opponent's belt, and oshi, which revolves around slapping or thrusting. The most commonly used winning technique is yori-kiri, which literally means "end the match by leaning on your opponent." The best way to execute this move is to grab the opponent's belt with both hands and simply drive them backwards over the rope. Extra force can result in the defeated wrestler crashing onto his back, in which case the move becomes yori-taoshi: "lean on and knock over." The most prevalent oshi technique is the simple oshi dashi, literally "push out," which involves applying heavy pressure to an opponent's chest with the palms and sending them over the rope. Should the opponent fall onto his back the move becomes oshi taoshi: "push and knock down." Similar winning moves come in the form of tsuki-dashi and tsuki-otoshi, the tsuki referring not to continuous pressure on the opponent's body but short, sharp thrusts which send them reeling. The hand-speed and venom demonstrated by the best tsuki artists can often be breathtaking, with one 1980s legend named Terao capable of landing three blows every second.

A wrestler tries a yori-kiri on his opponent

Exceptionally strong wrestlers may try throwing an opponent. The most popular throw is uwatenage, where the attacker grabs the belt from outside his opponent's defenses and swings him down. Shitatenage, meanwhile, involves latching onto the belt from inside the other fighter's defenses and upending him. Various pulls and twist forms of uwate and shitate exist, while other throws include: kubinage (from the neck), sukuinage (scooping from under an opponent's armpit) and kotenage (from clinching an arm and twisting it downwards). Even stronger wrestlers may try either tsuri-dashi (lifting an opponent over the ropes) or utchari (standing with your back to the ropes, lifting and spinning a foe simultaneously). It is here that we truly understand why size isn't everything in this most intriguing sport. Most of the exponents of throws and lifts are in the lighter category of wrestlers. In the 1990s, two formidable lightweights named Mainoumi and Kyokudozan sometimes threw down wrestlers 100 kilograms (220 lbs) heavier than themselves.

The sumo rankings chart, the banzuke, consists of six divisions: jonokuchi (entry level), jonidan (second grade), sandanme (third grade), makushita (below the curtain), juryo (the first salaried division) and makuuchi ("the elite inside the curtain"). References to curtains allegedly date back to the Edo era, when the best wrestlers were screened off by curtains while waiting their turn to fight – the rank-and-file standing outside for all to see. The bottom division of jonokuchi can only be entered after participation in an unlisted sumo qualification class known as mae-zumo. (A special exception is made for college or university sumo champions, who can actually join at third-division level). Some wrestlers, such as the current Bulgarian champion Kotooshu, can progress through the six divisions in as little as 10-12 tournaments. Others such as Kirishima, the first sumo wrestler ever to pen an active memoir, may take 40 tournaments or more. The vast majority of wrestlers, however, will never even make the second division, while more than 50% of sumo's new recruits are not even expected to last a year. Let the sport's simplicity not mask the gritty reality that sumo training is among the most punishing imaginable.

The lower ranks of the top division are classified as maegashira ("head of the rank-and-file"). Above maegashira are the sanyaku grades, a common term given to the highest-ranked employees of any sizeable organization.

Originally, as the name suggests (san meaning "three" in Japanese) sanyaku consisted of just three ranks: komusubi (junior champion), sekiwake (on the verge of champion status) and ozeki (champion). However, in the 1890s, an ozeki named Nishinoumi complained about being squeezed into the wings of the ranking chart and demanded he be given a separate ranking of yokozuna. The name literally means "horizontal belt," which is exactly what yokozuna are entitled to wear upon attaining the rank. Wrestlers at juryo and makuuchi level are allowed their own ring entrance ceremonies on tournament matchdays during which participants wear luxurious silk aprons gifted to them by fan clubs and sponsors. The yokozuna, meanwhile, is so revered that he is entitled to a separate ring-entrance ceremony by himself during which he sports not only the silk apron but the magnificent, knotted, white yokozuna belt, tied into either one large loop or two at the back depending on his training stable's tradition.

The rules for promotion and demotion are simple. More wins than losses in a given tournament entails promotion; the opposite entails demotion. Barring exceptional circumstances, this system more or less holds true from entry level until the rank of sekiwake. A sekiwake seeking ozeki status must win over 70% of his bouts over three consecutive tournaments, while an ozeki wishing to become yokozuna must generally win two tournaments in a row. Such is the revered status accorded to ozeki that he can only be demoted after two successive losing scores. Yokozuna status, on the other hand, is considered an honor so outstanding that it should never be sullied with a losing score. Should that event occur, and there have only been two instances since World War Two, the yokozuna is immediately expected to resign. Of course, a yokozuna is expected to have the dignity to accept that his weakened body may embarrass him, and retire before that fear becomes a reality.

The sport is, of course, coated in an intriguing layer of Shinto customs that distinctly separate it from other combat forms. The solid-clay ring or dohyo is purified by a referee dressed as a Shinto priest the day before each tournament, while wrestlers in the top two divisions (and the third, if time permits) repeatedly purify the dohyo themselves by sprinkling salt prior to a match. Wrestlers also stamp the ground prior to combat to ensure that evil spirits are scared away or even trampled upon.

[2]
ORIGINS

The origins of sumo are, as with most sports with a long history, unclear. Historians have noted similarities with ancient Korean wrestling and Mongolian grappling, which might explain why the Mongols have dominated sumo in recent years. The Japanese, however, fiercely proud of their culture, would never countenance any suggestion that sumo was invented outside of their land. Traditionalists will point to two historical texts, the Kojiki and the Nihon Shoki as evidence of sumo having been made by the Japanese for the Japanese.

Japan's earlier years are popularly believed to have been presided over by the Yamato clan. Yamato imagery still has an incredibly strong influence over Japanese culture today, providing inspiration not only for a successful children's series and movie, but also the name of the 2011 women's world soccer champions: Nadesico Japan ("Japanese flowers of Yamato"). It is little surprise, then, that sumo – the national sport (kokugi) of Japan – is also closely related to Yamato. According to the Kojiki, Yamato's very right to rule was determined by a sumo-style wrestling match. A deity representing Yamato faced off against the son of the ruler of Izumo, and soundly defeated him.

The legend surrounding the first ever sumo match also concerns Yamato and Izumo. The Nihon Shoki maintains that Izumo's warrior Nominosukune was pitted against Taimanokehaya of Yamato in a fight to the death. The description of the match is highly brutal, with Nominosukune not only throwing his opponent down but kicking him repeatedly until his ribs cracked into his lungs. It is truly amazing that a sport renowned for its dignity and emotional restraint would have (allegedly) begun in such a brutal and barbaric way. Yet more astonishing was that Nominosukune, upon winning the match for Izumo, then meekly pledged his services to the Emperor Suinin of Yamato, thus allowing Yamato to continue its hold on power. With Suinin's very existence being disputed, doubts have been cast on the validity of the entire story, but the legend has proved so romantic and popular that it has formed the subject of fine scroll paintings and given birth to several shrines named after Nominosukune. One such shrine is located in reasonable walking distance of the national sumo hall and contains a giant stone tablet listing every wrestler to have been promoted to the highest rank.

The general message of such mythical bouts is that sumo can somehow be connected to the "will of the deities." Hence did sumo embrace the customs of Shinto, which literally translates as "Path of the Gods." The sprinkling of salt and stamping of feet before a match, the purification of the mouth with "power water," the consecration of the ring by a referee dressed as a Shinto priest, the blanket ban on women touching the dohyo, and the inauguration of grand champions at Tokyo's Meiji Shrine are all shining examples of sumo's stern commitment to upholding Shinto values.

Historical evidence suggests that competitive sumo was first performed before aristocrats in seventh-century Japan, at the courts of the rulers from Nara city. It bore striking resemblance to the courtyard wrestling festivals staged by Chinese elites before that. The following Heian period (794-1195) saw the sport extend to the masses and, according to historian W.G. Beesley, become a popular spectator sport. In 587, the conquest of Japan by the Soga clan saw Buddhism adopted as the new state religion, thus placing added importance on sumo as a bastion of Shinto values, and was frequently performed before emperors highly sympathetic to its values.

As the Heian period progressed, and the battle-hardened samurai class developed, sumo gained a new lease of life as a military training exercise. Even today, sumo wrestlers are referred to as "The Last of the Samurai," their living link to this long lost age represented by the samurai-style topknots into which their hair is carefully tied.

It was during the Edo period that sumo truly became a sport of the masses – in some cases to a dangerous extent. At one stage, impromptu sumo contests in the street were attracting rowdy crowds and authorities began to issue edicts banning such public performances. To increase the legitimacy of such edicts, it was decided that a professional sumo association be established with an official rankings system. That decision was made round about 1757, when the first official rankings chart or banzuke was published by the sumo elder named Negishi (unofficial woodblock banzuke having been around for the previous 60 years). Even today, two and a half centuries on, the highly artistic Japanese script used to write wrestlers' names, birthplaces and ranks on the banzuke is known as "Negishi script." Since 1926 it has become custom for a senior referee to produce the entire ranking list by hand – a process which is said to take about two weeks. The banzuke's paramount importance is underlined by the fact that every sumo training stable puts their wrestler's current rank on the wall above the training area, motivating them to work harder and climb higher.

The first banzuke are illuminating for several reasons. Firstly, the highest rank at the time was listed as ozeki – yokozuna would not be officially codified for another 133 years. Secondly, they clearly indicate the wrestlers who held favor with the warlords of the day, and those who did not. Some wrestlers were simply brought in at the rank of ozeki by a powerful patron despite never having fought competitive bouts before. Two wrestlers particularly favored by the power-brokers were Tanikaze and Onogawa, whose achievements continue to be spoken about today. These two were the first wrestlers to receive the honorary title of yokozuna, conferred by the ultra-powerful Yoshida family, who were solely responsible for awarding yokozuna licenses until 1950. Yet, for all their fine wrestling skills, it remains little mentioned that Tanikaze and Onogawa sometimes dropped from ozeki to sekiwake, yet still kept their yokozuna license nonetheless. On the other hand, a gargantuan warrior by the name of Raiden, believed to be the strongest sumo wrestler ever lived, was never granted yokozuna status – presumably because his sponsor had no strong connection with the Yoshidas.

Record-breaking honors at the time belonged to Tanikaze, who won 62 consecutive bouts – a feat which remained unsurpassed for 157 years. Unsurprisingly, Onogawa was the man who ended the winning run, but Tanikaze quickly bounced back by posting another 43 consecutive victories. The chain of events even led to suspicions that Tanikaze had fixed this match, with one source even claiming he admitted this. There are many wonderful stories surrounding the Tanikaze-Onogawa rivalry, which to this day is credited with delivering sumo to genuine national prominence. On 11th June 1791, the two performed the day's final match before the 11th Tokugawa Shogun. Onogawa clearly wasn't ready to start the match and failed even to rise off his starter's line before Tanikaze clattered him. Whereas it is perfectly legitimate for a wrestler to call matta ("wait a sec!") while he readies himself for action, Onogawa apparently failed to do so and was swiftly judged the loser by a pro-Tanikaze official. The Shogun was bitterly disappointed at the anticlimactic end to the day and allegedly called for a re-match, but for some reason officials were able to ignore his authority. No winning technique was given. Instead, Onogawa was adjudged to have lost by kimake – "defeated by one's own mind." Tanikaze, meanwhile, was given a bow by the shogun, which he promptly spun above his head. The bow-twirling ceremony, which currently takes place at the end of every tournament match day, is said to date from this event.

Edo Japan also saw the birth and growth of ukiyo-e woodblock prints as a popular art form, especially so in sumo circles. Tanikaze and Onogawa were prime ukiyo-e material and their prints were tailor-made for the rank-and-file sumo follower who could not afford a full painting of a wrestler and craved a cheaper, mass-produced alternative. Customers from outside the cities were attracted by prints that depicted the outcome of important matches and, from 1757, copies of the banzuke. As a result, images of grappling sumo greats surrounded by rowdy crowds in outdoor stadia proliferated. The general impression generated is that sumo wrestlers, by virtue of their sheer size and strength, were completely awe-inspiring at that time, and generated mass excitement by their presence. Many of these wonderful prints, including especially fine ones by the revered Utagawa family, can regularly be seen on display in the art museum of Tokyo's New Otani Hotel, itself founded by a former sumo wrestler who was wealthy enough to buy hoards of ukiyo-e classics.

After the Meiji Restoration brought an end to 265 years of Shogun control in 1867-8, sumo gained an unexpected boost from the new emperor, despite the fact Japan was heavily focused on modernization at the expense of tradition. Although the samurai were liquidated in 1871, sumo was hailed as the ultimate symbol of the country Japan wanted to become: (fukoku kyohei – a great country with a strong military). Shinto was suddenly declared the new Japanese state's national religion, and Emperor Meiji was adamant that every male schoolchild partake in sumo lessons. Such a policy certainly built up sumo's potential fan numbers, and was continued by subsequent emperors. Indeed, Emperor Hirohito even practiced amateur sumo himself, and simply adored sumo, forever gracing tournament matchdays with his presence and introducing the Emperor's Cup for tournament winners.

The turn of the 20th century saw the emergence of two highly dominant yokozuna, Umegatani and Hitachiyama, who brought the sport's popularity to new levels. A statue of the two in battle can still be seen at Tokyo's Yasukuni Shrine today. Hitachiyama was a truly formidable figure whose influence extended far beyond the ring. In 1907 he became the first sumo wrestler ever to visit the White House and even performed a ring-entering ceremony for President Theodore Roosevelt. He was also the first sumo wrestler to stand for elected office and also helped build the first national sumo hall or kokugikan. (When asked as to what he would provide as collateral for a loan, he allegedly showed the bank manager his bulging muscles!) Alas, once the Ume-Hitachi boom ended, sumo fell on tough times, especially when the kokugikan burned to cinders in 1917 and a typhoon blew down the reconstruction attempt. By the early 1920s, sumo executives were unable to properly pay their wrestlers, leading to a mini strike and lock-in at a factory in Tokyo's Mikawajima district. The most viable way to avert further financial strife was for the Tokyo and Osaka Sumo Associations to pool their resources, forming the first all-Japan Sumo Association in 1925.

In January and February 1932, the new sumo association was almost brought to its knees by an even bigger wrestlers' strike. Led by the sekiwake Tenryu, 32 top-division wrestlers handed in their resignations en masse and tried to form a breakaway organization with limited success. However, with sponsors and local authorities remaining loyal to the official sumo authorities (the latter by conveniently refusing permits for breakaway wrestlers to stage tournaments) the striking movement forever suffered from lack of funds and the absence of a permanent home. The official sumo association was even able to buy off some of the strikers by acceding to demands over wage and pension reform, meaning that by the late-1930s it survived while the rebel movement faded into oblivion. The incident remains, to this day, the closest the Japan Sumo Association has come to crumbling. As the rifts from the strike healed, sumo re-established its crowd-pulling potential with the exploits of fearsome grand champion Tamanishiki, handsome Musashiyama and his competent rival Minanogawa.

The years immediately prior to World War Two were electrified by the lightweight legend Futabayama, who was actually blind in one eye but never revealed this handicap publicly until after the war. Starting in 1936, this immensely gifted technician embarked upon an all-time record-winning run of 69 consecutive bouts. As there were only two tournaments a year at that time, Futabayama actually remained unbeaten for three years. When he was finally upended by Akinoumi in 1939 the sumo hall literally went crazy with spectators hurling everything they could find into the ring – including oranges! The radio commentator even became so confused as to mix up left and right when describing the winning move. With war taking a heavy effect on the sumo schedule (at one stage the sumo hall itself was requisitioned by Allied Forces) Futabayama's fighting days were cruelly limited. He returned briefly after the war but was a pale shadow of the fighter of yore and retired in 1946. His career over, he briefly went off the rails and beat up several policeman in an alcohol-fuelled rage while consorting with a lady who called herself the "Sun Goddess." However, he recovered from such troubles to take over the sumo association chairmanship in a time of crisis in 1958, and lead the sport he loved until his death 10 years later.

In the few years prior to his becoming chairman, sumo experienced its first major post-war boom. A new sumo hall was built in Kuramae, NHK television started covering matches live in 1951, and before long sumo was set alight by the fierce rivalry of two scintillating grand champions: Wakanohana and Tochinishiki. Sumo's first years on television were thus labeled the Waka-Tochi era. In 1957, Wakanohana's celebrity status was cemented when he became the first sumo star to appear in a movie about himself. He would later become a formidable sumo coach, training up two grand champions and one ozeki, before finishing his official career as a chairman of the association.

If the '50s belonged to Waka-Tochi then the '60s were certainly the Hakuho era. "Hakuho" was a compound word created by abbreviating the names of the leading grand champions at that time: Kashiwado and Taiho, who both earned promotion to yokozuna in September 1961. The two men subsequently collected 37 of the 61 tournament championships between January 1961 and January 1971 – an astonishing 32 of them going to Taiho, an all-time record which has yet to be broken. Although fans look back fondly on this so-called Sumo Golden Age, Taiho's domination was not so favorably received at the time, with several fans complaining of boring predictability and attendance dropping in the late 1960s. To this day, he remains part of the legendary "Big Three" '60s cultural icons: Taiho, Yomiuri Giants and Tamago-yaki. In the Hakuho era sumo found its way to the big screen via the 1967 James Bond classic: You Only Live Twice. However, when Sean Connery visits the sumo hall, he is greeted not by Taiho but by one of his rivals, Sadanoyama. The reason, observant fans may note, is that Sadanoyama happened to be the prize recruit and son-in-law of the sumo association chairman at that time – whose assent would have been required for any movie appearances by his members.

The 1970s began with the shock retirement of Taiho, whose unexpected loss to a lightweight muscleman named Takanohana convinced him that his body had weakened beyond repair. Takanohana never made yokozuna himself – simply because he smoked too much, according to the man himself – but he easily became the most popular sumo wrestler of the decade, earning the nickname "The Prince of Sumo." He also had the distinction of being trained by his (much) older brother, who happened to be the former yokozuna Wakanohana. Takanohana did collect two championships in March and September 1975, much to the delight of the nation and his vast army of female followers. However, the 1970s belonged to his defeated opponent in both those epic contests, the giant grand champion Kitanoumi, who is currently Chairman of the entire Sumo Association. Terrifying opponents with his 160-kilogram (352 lbs) bulk, Kitanoumi was promoted to sumo's highest rank at just 21 years of age and eventually amassed 24 championships – second only to Taiho at that time. His most fascinating rivalry was with the handsome, side-burned Wajima, who collected 12 tournament titles himself and eventually ended up broke and scraping together a living as a pro-wrestler. To this day, Wajima remains the only sumo wrestler fighting under his real family name to have attained yokozuna status.

The 1980s began with the retirements of Wajima and Takanohana, and the emergence of a new Prince of Sumo to take their place: Chiyonofuji. This incredibly agile and muscular lightweight endured a difficult route to the top, yo-yoing between the second and third divisions before finally hitting peak form 11 years after he joined the sport. There was nothing in the entire previous decade which suggested he would dominate sumo in the 1980s, but rise to prominence he did, collecting an incredible 31 of the 60 top-division championships on offer between January 1981 and November 1990. Nicknamed "Wolf" for his fierce glare, he not only symbolized the spirit of a nation enjoying an economic boom but set a then-post-war record of 53 consecutive victories in 1988. It should have been far more, but he unexpectedly lost the final match of Emperor Hirohito's reign to the giant Onokuni, a frequently underperforming grand champion who was even told by his own coach that he had no chance of winning, and consequently got up extra early the next day to work out a game plan and make sure he did! In July 1989, Chiyonofuji made further history by taking on his own stablemate Hokutoumi in a playoff – the first time that two yokozuna from the same stable had met in the ring. Of course, he won.

Within three years though, the face of sumo would change completely as the old forces of power were swept away. Chiyonofuji and Hokutoumi both retired within a year of each other, while fellow yokozuna Onokuni and Asahifuji also hung up their sashes. Never before had so many grand champions retired in quick succession, leaving a colossal gap at the top of the rankings chart destined to be filled by an entirely new breed of fighter.

[3]

MODERN DAY SUMO

In the present-day, sumo tournaments are staged six times a year: one for every odd month. The January, May and September meets occur in the Ryogoku Kokugikan, an 11000-capacity arena purpose-built for Japan's national sport. The March, July and November meets take place in the cities of Osaka, Nagoya and Fukuoka respectively. Each tournament lasts 15 days. The top two divisions fight every day while wrestlers in the bottom four divisions fight seven matches staggered over the fortnight. The wrestler who garners more victories than anybody else in his division will take the championship for that level. Should two or more wrestlers tie for the lead after their final matches, a sudden-death playoff system comes into effect, with the winner taking the top prize. Wrestlers with narrow winning scores (4-3 in the bottom divisions and 8-7 at the top level) will likely earn small promotions for the following tourney, while wrestlers with big winning scores (6-1 or 11-4) will usually leap up the rankings chart. The opposite applies to wrestlers with losing scores. As in western league-style sports, a promotion-relegation system between divisions is in place.

The tone for modern-day sumo was undoubtedly set by the exploits of an oversized teenager from Hawaii named Jesse Kuhaulua, who journeyed to Japan as a 19-year-old in 1963. After nine years of hard graft in sumo's notoriously unforgiving training system, Kuhaulua – under the ring name of Takamiyama – became the first non-Japanese ever to claim the top-division championship, in July 1972. Kuhaulua's successes, and highly persuasive recruiting techniques in his native Hawaii, paved the way for sumo to take on a more international flavor and ultimately triggered the downfall of Japanese domination.

One of the many Hawaiians recruited by Takamiyama was Salevaa Atisanoe (b.1963) who joined professional sumo in 1982 and raced to the top division in just two years. Forever gaining weight rapidly, he earned something of a behemoth's reputation under the ring name Konishiki, which ironically means "small brocade." His regular fighting weight was 235 kilograms (518 lbs) and peaked at over 270 (595 lbs). Serving up a succession of all-out thrusting attacks, Konishiki not only collected the runner-up honors in his first top division tournament but ultimately became the first non-Japanese to make sumo's second rank of ozeki in 1987. Four years later, he became the first foreigner to win two top-division tournaments, following that up with a third championship success which led to calls for his promotion to yokozuna level. He was denied promotion in controversial circumstances that many Americans pinned on xenophobia. This was not strictly true. Weight-induced knee problems were just as much to blame.

Indeed, the first foreigner to become yokozuna was not Konishiki but another man recruited by Takamiyama and – unlike Konishiki – directly trained by him. This Hawaiian's name was Chadwick Rowan (b.1969) better known in sumo circles as the 204-centimetre Akebono. Initially riding the cusp of Konishiki's wave, Akebono went on to outperform his heavier compatriot and win two successive championships in November 1992 and January 1993. He was joined on sumo's highest rank by another Hawaiian, Fiamalu Penitani (ring name: Musashimaru), in July 1999. Together, Akebono and Musashimaru would engage in a fiercely competitive rivalry with the Japanese siblings Masaru and Koji Hanada, far better known as Wakanohana and Takanohana, sons of the 1970s Prince of Sumo and the first brothers to hold sumo's highest rank simultaneously. Sumo was indeed completely dominated by these four names for the best part of ten years.

After the Big Four faded away in quick succession between 2000 and 2002, sumo's torch was passed to the next generation of foreign wrestlers, most of who were recruited after 1998 – the year in which a five-year ban on enrollment of non-Japanese was relaxed. Gone

were the oversized Hawaiians of yore. In was
the new breed of athletic and nimble fighter
from Mongolia, a nation with a proud and dis-
tinguished grappling history waiting patiently
to take sumo by storm. Mongolia's first claim
to dominance came in the form of Asashoryu
Akinori (b.1980), who entered the Japanese
education system at 15, became a high school
champion and then earned yokozuna status at
the tender age of 22.

*Yokozuna Asashoryu performing his ring en-
tering ceremony, January 2009*

Vicious with his thrusts and lethal on the belt, Asashoryu pulled virtually every technique imaginable in destroying the Japanese field around him, becoming the first wrestler to win every tournament in a calendar year in the process. From 2003-2006 he was almost unstoppable, setting records left, right and centre, including that for most victories in a calendar year: 84 from 90 bouts. Injuries and personal problems soon caught up with him though and – like Konishiki before him – saw his trailblazing exploits cruelly outdone by a compatriot. That man's name was Hakuho Sho (b.1985), the son of an Olympic freestyle-wrestling gold medalist.

Hakuho, who stands 192 centimeters and weighs around 150 kilograms (330 lbs), boasted a superior physique to Asashoryu and started to defeat him regularly from 2007. In May of that year, he gained yokozuna status himself and in 2009 he defeated Asashoryu in all six of their regulation matches (albeit losing two championship playoffs to him). 2009 also saw Hakuho eclipse Asashoryu's win-record with 86 successes from 90 bouts, an astonishing feat which he even repeated the following year. Hakuho then also equaled his compatriot's record of seven successive tournament wins in 2011. His most remarkable year was actually 2010 when he embarked upon an incredible winning streak that ran for 63 matches – a post-war record and the second-longest ever. Between 2002 and 2011, an eye-popping 46 out

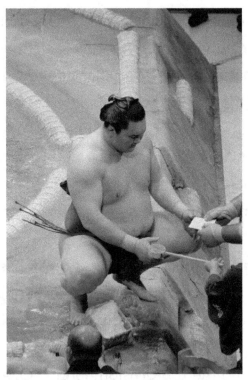

Hakuho prepares himself for a match, January 2012

of 60 tournaments were collected by
Asashoryu and Hakuho alone, a level of domination completely unprecedented in sumo.
With Asashoryu now out of the way, Hakuho
has a fantastic chance to overhaul the all-time
landmark for championship wins, the 32 set by
the Taiho in 1970.

Other Mongolians who have made their
mark include the comparatively slender
Harumafuji (b.1984) who has already won two
tournaments – more than any other person currently on the second rank. The similarly-built
Kakuryu (b.1986) looks destined to join
Harumafuji on the second rank in future. Both
men are highly agile and dangerous on the
belt.

The Mongolian ascent has given rise to a
situation deemed unthinkable throughout hun-
dreds of years of sumo history: that six years
could pass without a single Japanese wrestler
collecting the top-division honors. Ozeki
Tochiazuma was the last man to do so in January 2006, and even he has long since retired.

Every championship is marked by a portrait of the winner commissioned by the Mainichi Newspaper. Every portrait commissioned in the last five years is hung up in the Kokugikan, and 2011 marked the first time that all of these portraits depicted a foreigner, much to the consternation of a fiercely patriotic Japanese media.

But it is not only Mongolians who have been changing sumo's face. The Europeans have also blossomed since the mid-2000s. Giant Georgian Kokkai stormed into the first division in late-2003, while balding Russian pair Roho and Hakurozan became the first non-Japanese siblings to make the top level in 2005. Later that year, a towering Bulgarian with a powerlifter's physique became the first European to earn an ozeki promotion. His name was Kaloyan Mahlyanov (b.1983), otherwise known as Kotooshu. In May 2008, the 203-centimetre Kotooshu rewrote two millennia of sumo history by becoming the first European to collect the top-division championship. Many expected him to push on for yokozuna status, but injuries and the home comforts of a stable ozeki income seem to have jarred his progress. A more likely contender for Europe's inaugural yokozuna appears to be the massive Estonian Karel Hoovelson (b.1984), who in January 2012 became the second European to win an entire tournament. Hoovelson's ring name is Baruto, a Japanese pun on his "Baltic" origins. He is the only blond-haired tournament winner in sumo history and boasts an intimidating 198-centimetre, 185-kilogram (407 lbs) physique.

Baruto warms up, January 2012

The runner-up honors in January 2012 were shared by another European in the 200-kilogram (440 lbs) form of Gagamaru, from Georgia, thus underlining the great strides occidental wrestlers have made. His younger and more muscular compatriot, Tochinoshin (b.1987), has also flirted with the sanyaku ranks and could rise higher if niggling injuries can be overcome.

Outside of Georgia, Russia, Estonia and Mongolia, wrestlers from other nationalities have also enjoyed considerable success in recent years, not least Korean-born Kasugao and Chinese-born Sokokurai. Both, however, were fired in 2011 for alleged conspiracy to fix matches.

At present, it is difficult to find a Japanese wrestler with enough brute strength, tactical nous and coolness under pressure to arrest the surge in foreign domination. For a brief period in 2011, there were no Japanese men ranked in the top two ranks at all – for only the second time since the rankings system began in 1757. There are currently two Japanese on the second rank, both of whom have been runner-up in a tournament but not actually won one. The older man, Kotoshogiku (b.1984) is a highly competent belt-fighter but lacks the technical repertoire to rise higher. Japan's best hope clearly lies with the 190-centimetre, 160-kilogram (352 lbs) Kisenosato (b.1986) who has defeated Asashoryu and Hakuho on numerous occasions and exhibits an iron will to succeed.

Salaries in the top two divisions can scarce be described as high relative to other sports, but certainly entitle wrestlers to a standard of living in the top 2% of Japanese society. A consistent second division wrestler can expect to take home around $100,000 a year for his efforts while the yokozuna can expect to amass triple that amount. However, real money can be made from the numerous appearances, ranking and victory bonuses awarded by the sumo association, and the cash prizes (kensho) put up by sponsors on leading matches. In a December 2010 interview, Brazilian Kaisei stated he received over $18000 dollars for winning the second division tournament the previous month. The top-division tournament winner, meanwhile, will pocket over five times as much. Also in December 2010, Yokozuna Hakuho revealed that his total kensho money for the year amounted to $600,000. Considering that some of his 10-second matches were attracting $15000 in kensho alone, that can hardly be described as a bad hourly rate, especially when compared to the low wages he would have earned back home in Mongolia. Every wrestler enters a win-bonus system from the very moment they post their first winning score in the bottom division, but the points can only be converted into cash once he reaches a salaried level (i.e. the second division). Racking up points via winning scores, upsetting a yokozuna, garnering a special prize for Fighting Spirit, Technique or Outstanding Performance, making sanyaku, or collecting a tournament championship can pay real dividends, as the equivalent cash sum is paid to the rikishi in every subsequent tournament in which he competes.

In the 21st century, sumo is not only confined to the professional dohyo, however. Over 80 countries are currently affiliated to the International Sumo Federation, each boasting a crop of amateur sumo wrestlers who are unbound by Shinto rituals, simply focusing on bouts and techniques. Whereas Shinto rituals prevent them from even touching a professional dohyo, women are freely allowed to compete in amateur sumo, with some heavyweights even tipping the scales at 200 kilograms (440 lbs). Participation of women is essential if sumo is to be installed as an Olympic sport. A concerted campaign has been in place for several years to secure sumo's Olympic status but has frequently hit the buffers due to opposition from the Japan Sumo Association, which perceives that a version of the sport that eschews Shinto beliefs would have no meaning at all. Asked in April 2006 whether sumo would ever become an Olympic sport, Hawaiian yokozuna Musashimaru told a gathering of world amateurs: "No, I don't think so. And if it does hit the Olympics, I'll enter!"

Sumo's present-day popularity can hardly be compared to the booms of the 1950s, 1980s and 1990s, and particularly noticeable is the lack of young people willing to become wrestlers. In 1998, the number was put at around 2000. In the summer of 2007, though, zero applicants applied. The total number of rikishi was noticeably dropping year on year even before 23 of them were fired in the scandals of 2011. Yet, the sumo association has developed some creditable marketing ploys, including all manner of sumo souvenirs, a new mascot for children and bento lunchboxes that contain top wrestlers' favorite foods. Sumo wrestlers are also popular guests on TV shows, and have recently started blogs and Facebook pages to reach out to the next generation on the web.

[4]

LIFE OF A MODERN-DAY SUMO WRESTLER

Every sumo wrestler must belong to a training stable in which he can learn his trade from a master, in this case a sumo coach, Edo-style. For all the emphasis placed on a matchday, the stable is where they will spend 90% of their sumo life, and fight 99% of their sumo bouts.

On a regular day, the junior sumo wrestler will awake in the small hours, between 0430 and 0530, to ensure the stable's practice ring is ready for the morning session. The dirt and sand used to protect the soles of a wrestler's feet from the harsh clay training surface will have been carefully scraped into a mound in the centre of the ring, and must be spread around the dohyo with straw brooms once more before the next practice begins. Towels and water are carefully laid out for the still-sleeping seniors, and a futon is dutifully prepared for the coach – who may also still be in bed. The coach will sit and watch proceedings from a raised area next to the practice ring called the agari-zashiki. Junior coaches will assist him either by shouting out instructions from the sidelines or, if they are young enough, donning a practice belt themselves and joining in.

The younger wrestlers commence practice between 0600 and 0700, with or without a watching junior coach. (One exceptionally dedicated wrestler explained how he secretly went out for a six-kilometer run even before training started!) They begin with some basic foot stamping to strengthen leg muscles, ranging anywhere from 30 to 300 repetitions. Novices in the background will be taking things more easily, performing limited shiko to strengthen their legs and playing catch with a heavy rice bag to build-up arm strength. They may also thrust a large wooden teppo pole in the corner of the training area to increase their thrusting power and skill. They will also practice how to move across the dohyo, their backs and knees slightly bent, their feet carefully opened out, their sliding forward movements carefully pronounced. Flexibility of the legs is increased by an excruciating exercise known as matawari (literally: doing the splits). The exercise involves sitting on the ground, widening the chunky legs and pressing not only one's chest but one's nose to the floor in front of them. Youngsters inevitably have trouble stretching so far and are thus sat upon by senior wrestlers – most of whom will weigh more than 130 kilograms (286 lbs) – until their joints crack into a more flexible form. Those who doubt the flexibility of a sumo wrestler should observe this exercise carefully.

Basic training exercises at all levels are as follows. Suri-ashi hones the skill of advancing across the ring with defensive and offensive hand movements, either by accentuated strides or grinding the soles of one's feet painfully across the solid clay. Butsukari-geiko sees one wrestler "lend his chest" to an opponent and invite him to charge full-bloodedly. The aim is for the charging wrestler to force the chest-lender over the rope, perhaps five or six times in succession. Easier said than done when the opponent weighs 140 kilograms (308 lbs). Should he fail to complete the task, he will be asked to charge yet more, sometimes until he collapses with exhaustion and is taken outside to be sloshed with water. Another chest-lending exercise sees a wrestler attempt to move another out of the ring by thrusting. The most intensive exercise is, of course, the practice bout. Stables institute a system called moshi-ai geiko, whereby the winner of the first practice match fights a succession of opponents until he is defeated. Other wrestlers are supposed to watch each practice match and hurriedly run up to the winner, begging to be fought next. If they seem a little overzealous, this is because they know they will receive a beating from their coach if they fail to show enough enthusiasm. The unwritten rule is that wrestlers must be punished in some way for perceived underperformance, perhaps through a thwack with a bamboo cane, a timely punch to the head, or simply enforced repetition of particular exercises. Sumo's received wisdom is that to train fighters who are fearless and fiercely determined to go the extra mile, such training is a prerequisite.

Sumo traditionally shunned any form of dedicated weight training, clinging to the traditional romantic image of men growing strong simply by practicing with each other, repeating standard exercises and lifting random heavy objects within reach. "Lifting weights is a waste of time," was how the stablemaster of ex-ozeki Kirishima once put it. "You'd be far better off practicing your shiko stamps." However, in the 1970s, secret weight training sessions among younger wrestlers began to take off, especially among those seeking to overcome a lack of natural bulk. Kirishima recalls being surprised when he first entered the gym upon seeing regular office workers bench pressing 20-kilograms (44 lbs) more than he could. The image shocked him into becoming the most fanatic weight trainer in sumo, and at the time of his ozeki promotion he could benchpress more than 200 kilograms (440 lbs). Nowadays, all sumo stables have a supply of weights while some newer ones, like Shikoroyama (run by a stablemate of Kirishima) even have purpose-built gyms inside. The fiery grand champion Asashoryu was once filmed bench-pressing 300 kilograms (661 lbs)!

Training is followed by a chanko lunch, prepared with the help of the junior wrestlers, who must practice their cooking skills as part of their sumo responsibilities. Some of them who fail to make the grade as fighters either join or open their own chanko restaurants after retiring from the sport. Chanko is a mixture of a soup and a stew. The base for the soup can be salt, soy sauce or miso paste, while the ingredients usually comprise of vegetables, chicken and fish. There is no set chanko cooking style and every stable can vary according to the coach's preferences. Interestingly, two-legged animals such as chicken are specifically chosen because they symbolize a man standing on two feet – therefore a winning pose in a sumo match. Four-legged animals are supposed to symbolize a man upended on the sumo dohyo, and are thus deemed both unlucky and unusable for sumo chanko. Side dishes are available in abundance, with salads, omelets, croquettes and fried cutlets frequently on the menu.

Morning side dishes at Minezaki Stable, January 2008

Eating is done in order of seniority, meaning the junior wrestlers must first act as waiters for the seniors and any patrons or friends who are invited to dine with them. Only after the seniors have eaten – and usually pilfered the most succulent bits – can the youngsters sit down for their own meals. Youngsters are expected to eat heavily to gain weight quickly, and will work their way through several bowls of rice. One 1980s wrestler named Ozutsu claimed that he was shoveling down 10 bowls of rice a meal to gain the necessary pounds. After the dishes have been washed, the junior wrestlers head to their stable's dormitory for a nap to convert calories into fat. The seniors, meanwhile, either head to their private rooms or, if they are earning enough, private apartments for some chill-out time.

The afternoon schedule is far less regulated than the morning. Some fitness fanatics might head to the gym or use some exercise bikes that their stable has bought. Others will simply read magazines and comics, or update their Facebook pages. Others might head out into downtown Tokyo for a game of pachinko – a strikingly popular pastime among the sumo community. If the weather permits, wrestlers may don baseball gloves and head into the streets for a game of catch. Many junior wrestlers are assigned a senior wrestler to attend to, and must fetch any magazines or drinks he calls for, in addition to running general errands.

Juniors must also carry out chores for the stable management, and unluckier ones will be asked to go shopping for elderly mothers of stablemasters! As the evening draws in, junior wrestlers might head to a convenience store, takeaway or cheap ramen shop to buy food with some of their monthly allowance money. High-level wrestlers, on the other hand, will likely be invited to dine out at more expensive restaurants with patrons or sponsors.

Training is at its most intense during the fortnight preceding a tournament, but tapers off once the competitive action starts. Training on tournament matchdays is generally viewed as a chance for wrestlers to complete a basic warm-up before their matches, although some may undertake specific preparation for a big fight, either perfecting a specific technique or asking a stablemate to imitate a particular opponent's style. Practice sessions usually begin later during these weeks, about 0700 or 0800, and many stablemasters are unable to attend, instead carrying out their duties at the actual sumo hall. It is thus the case that mid-tournament training sessions sometimes carry a comical tone, with a junior wrestler nervously on standby at the stable door on the lookout for a returning coach, while his stablemates scarcely bother to train at all – on one occasion even playing catch with salt crystals! It is doubly funny, of course, to see the wrestlers immediately spring into a more serious pose the moment the coach returns!

The training area at a sumo stable

On matchdays, junior wrestlers will head to the sumo hall as early as 0730 in preparation for early morning matches. Those whose stables are situated near to the hall will walk, the clop-clop of their clogs a signature theme of the Ryogoku sumo district. Wrestlers whose stables lie further away from the action will take the train, overpowering entire carriages with the strong scent of the bintzuke oil used to lacquer their hair. When their matches have finished, they pack up their mini kitbags and head to a cheap Japanese restaurant in the vicinity, or even the local McDonalds that offers wrestlers free meals if they present a sumo association scorecard that proves they won their day's bout. After that, they will return to the stable. Many wrestlers in the third and fourth divisions act as official attendants to the salaried wrestlers in their stable, meaning they will fight their matches later-morning or early-afternoon and then remain in the kokugikan. When the senior wrestler arrives in the early or mid-afternoon, the junior attendants will help him change, run mini errands and carry his luxurious floor cushion to ringside. Should the senior wrestler collect some prize money that day, he may filter some of it to his attendants. He may also invite them to dine with him at the expense of his patrons.

Sumo coaches are renowned for imposing strict night-time curfews on their charges. In 2011, one coach was reprimanded by his employers for using a golf-club to beat two wrestlers who went late-night drinking. Girlfriends should be kept discreet while marriages should only be confined to salaried-level wrestlers, in line with traditional Japanese thinking that a man with no income cannot expect a woman to provide for him.

Three times a year, wrestlers will leave their Tokyo stable environment behind when journeying to the Osaka, Nagoya and Fukuoka tournaments. Prior to these tournaments, the wrestlers must attend countryside tour events (jungyo) out in the open, with the juniors having to run yet more errands for the seniors, especially the carrying of food and drink. The jungyo sees wrestlers interact more closely with the fans, signing autographs, even sitting down to eat chanko with more fortunate ones. They will also stage practice matches and light-hearted contests to entertain the spectators. Most importantly, the jungyo can bring sumo to fans who either live too far from, or cannot afford to go to, an actual tournament venue. Once the countryside tours have finished, the stables head to either shrines or warehouses in the tournament city, and set up base there for three weeks or so.

The week after a tournament is a time for relaxing, either to head slowly back to Tokyo or to stay with family members or friends living near the tournament city. In Tokyo, meanwhile, the week after the January tournament is viewed as the year's most relaxed, with some foreign wrestlers journeying to their homelands while their stablemates meet friends or visit shrines for the traditional bean-throwing festival on February 3rd. Sumo wrestlers attend a variety of ceremonial events throughout the year, including wrestler retirement ceremonies, wrestler promotion parties, shrine visits, holding babies to symbolically "pass on strength," and pounding rice-cakes for the New Year.

Life in a sumo stable is certainly not for the faint-hearted. Every year recruits will slip away in the dead of night, unable to face any more grueling training sessions, where they are sometimes reduced to tears. However, those who have the mettle to survive will live with considerable financial security. Even non-salaried wrestlers receive sumo association monthly allowances, and have all their board and meals provided by their employers.

[5]

CURRENT CONTROVERSIES IN THE SPORT

The last five years have seen sumo en-meshed in an unprecedented number of scan-dals, partly due to more aggressive media reporting, partly due to more aggressive polic-ing of gangster activities.

Sumo's name was dragged into the mire in June 2007 when a 17-year-old novice at the Tokitsukaze training stable, Tokitaizan, was hospitalized after a training session and died of multiple injuries. Not only was he witnessed training hours after the original session fin-ished, but was also found to have cigarette burns on his body. Several wrestlers from Tokitsukaze stable, along with the stablemaster himself, were arrested under suspicion of causing his death through excess bullying. Under police questioning, the stablemaster admitted to having hit Tokitaizan over the head with a jagged, broken beer bottle in order to discipline him (albeit not on the day of his death). After the police were heavily criticized for the length of their investigation, they did manage to secure a conviction of Coach Tokitsukaze, who was jailed and lost his job.

Sumo found itself on the ropes again the following month when its notoriously tempestuous grand champion, Asashoryu of Mongolia, absented himself from the gruelling summer tour after presenting a doctor's certificate stating he had an injury. He was allowed to return home to Ulan Bator where, instead of recuperating, he was filmed wearing a Manchester United shirt and playing football with his friends. The sumo association was so enraged at his apparent feigning of injury to abscond from official duties that they gave him an unprecedented two-tournament suspension, and confined him to his home for several weeks. A shaken Asashoryu, depressed at having to wait six months for his next tournament action, allegedly started refusing to eat and spiraled into depression. The Japanese public, with a skeptical attitude towards mental illness, accused him of faking that condition also, and became even more enraged when the Japan Sumo Association Chairman, Kitanoumi, assented to Asashoryu's request to be treated for depression in his native Mongolia – thus seemingly earning another chance to party with his friends.

It was not the first time Asashoryu had irked sumo authorities. In 2003 he became the first grand champion ever to be disqualified from a match. His crime: pulling the hair of opponent Kyokushuzan, an apparent act of revenge for the controversial defeat Kyokushuzan had inflicted on him in the previous tournament. After the hair-pull, the two men reportedly squared up again in the dressing rooms – having to be physically restrained by other wrestlers – and then forced another altercation in the car park during which Asashoryu was said to break the car mirror of Kyokushuzan's patron. From that moment onwards, he was on thin ice, seemingly only spared the sack because he was the only grand champion and the biggest crowd puller. Once the sumo association produced a rival grand champion in Hakuho, Asashoryu would be allowed no more behavioral mishaps.

After Asashoryu mounted a dramatic comeback in 2008, only to miss the last two tournaments again due to a more genuine-looking injury, he enjoyed a respite from media scrutiny due to exploits of three Russian wrestlers: Roho, Hakurozan and Wakanoho. The latter was fired from sumo after his wallet was found to contain a marijuana sachet, thus in violation of Japan's zero-tolerance policy towards drugs. Brothers Roho and Hakurozan were then also accused of consuming recreational drugs and brutally fired without proof. Embarrassingly, Hakurozan belonged to the stable managed by Sumo Chairman Kitanoumi, who was thus forced to resign the top job. A fourth – Japanese – wrestler Wakakirin was also accused of drug-taking by the tabloids but spared investigation until early 2009, when he admitted wrongdoing and was also fired.

The following January, Asashoryu's fiery temper once again proved his undoing when – after two years of extensive public rehabilitation – he was caught on CCTV pursuing a man in the street, before reportedly chasing him into a taxi and breaking his cheekbone. The two were claimed to have disputed in a night-club beforehand and, although the victim oddly elected not to press charges, the sumo association were determined to make Asashoryu suffer. On February 4th, 2010, Asashoryu was summoned for a meeting with directors at which he was asked to voluntarily resign. He angrily refused to do so, causing some board members to explode and threaten to fire him without compensation – a sumo first. After being talked round by three senior association directors, Asashoryu accepted the need to retire and ultimately received a huge $1 million-plus payoff in recognition of the 25 tournament championships he collected – the highest number by any non-Japanese to date.

Just as sumo was reeling from the loss of its biggest star, it was hit by another storm at the end of the May tournament when Ozeki Kotomitsuki was accused of gambling millions of yen on baseball games – an illegal practice in Japan. Kotomitsuki initially denied the accusations but an investigation by police, which included seizures of rikishi mobile phones, later proved them to be true. Worse still, a string of senior wrestlers were also found to be heavily involved in gambling – most certainly with the aid of organized crime syndicates – leading to calls that a tournament be cancelled for the first time in 64 years. Further fuel was added to the flames with the revelation that the manager of Kise training stable had gifted several premium tickets to yakuza members so that they could be easily seen on TV by their colleagues in prison. The upshot: absolute turmoil that led to the liquidation of Kise stable and the resignation of Sumo Chairman Musashigawa, who was temporarily replaced by a Tokyo legal official. Kotomitsuki also became the first ozeki to be fired from sumo, while several other wrestlers and coaches received harsh demotions.

Incredibly, during this controversy the seeds were sewn for an even bigger scandal six months later. The reason for the time lag has never been explained, adding to suspicion that it was part of a concerted attack on sumo by the authorities. In January 2011, it was suddenly revealed by police that the mobile phones seized the previous year contained text messages that appeared to discuss match-fixing. Further wrestler phones were seized and further evidence was uncovered, thus bringing about the unthinkable: the cancellation of a tournament for the first time since World War Two. The timing of the revelations was particularly damaging, coming just weeks after the sumo association won a long-running defamation case against leading publishing house Kodansha for printing detailed match-fixing accusations in 2007. Part of Kodansha's case rested on the secret taping of a leading stablemaster who even named the days on which big names had fixed bouts. That evidence was dismissed on the grounds it was obtained by a jilted former girlfriend and – highly dubiously – on the coach's claim that he was talking nonsense under the influence of medication. Equally dubious, though, was the police's seeming nonchalance towards such evidence in their actual investigation, dragging up the names of numerous lower-rankers but not a single person from the upper echelons.

In the spring of 2011, no fewer than 25 sumo association members (23 wrestlers and two coaches) lost their jobs following the police investigation. Most of them angrily protested their innocence and complained that they were victims of a witch-hunt – but to no avail. The top-two divisions were shorn of a staggering 33% of their staff, leading to record numbers of promotions from the third division, thus opening new doors for rising stars. The official line was that a large number of wrestlers at the bottom of the second division were fixing matches because they were petrified of demotion and loss of salary. Evidence of an unusually high percentage of final-day victories gained by rikishi in need was used to support this. However, no media outlet touched on an even more striking statistic: that from March 2007- March 2011, the success record for Ozeki needing to win on the final day was 100%.

The match-fixing scandal unexpectedly provided a unique insight into sumo's cultural nuances. The investigation gave rise to two types of fixed match: yaocho (the payment of money to secure a result) and koi ni yatta mukiryoku zumo (deliberately going easy on an opponent without financial gain, knowing the favour will be repaid in future). The latter, while angrily condemned by some fans even on matchdays, is generally condoned in all aspects of Japanese culture, and – worst of all for sumo purists – is nigh-impossible to prove. Fines and public warnings do exist for perceived instances of underpowered sumo, but the practice has shown no signs of abating, even after the turbulent events of 2011.

CONCLUSION

The sumo association has gone to great lengths to stress that the match-fixing saga has been concluded, and that fans can look forward to genuine full-blooded contests in future.

While such statements may be dubious, the fact remains that the vast majority of sumo matches are – and always have been – real tests of strength.

The real tragedy of the bout-rigging scandal is that it has deflected attention from sumo's most pressing problems: the lack of home-grown talent at the top, the lack of schoolboys actually joining, and over-reliance on a highly aged fan base.

Sumo has confounded those who have predicted its demise before. With the right marketing approach, it can do so again.

CPSIA information can be obtained
at www.ICGtesting.com
Printed in the USA
BVHW072038141221
624005BV00022B/948